Beautiful

Passing

Lives

Beautiful
Passing
Lives

poems

by

Edward Harkness

Ed Harkness

Pleasure Boat Studio: A Literary Press
New York

Beautiful Passing Lives
Poems by Edward Harkness, ©2010

ISBN: 978-1-929355-73-0
Library of Congress Control Number: 2010915311

Cover Painting: "Room 322," by Sayaka Shigeta.
Photograph of cover art by Amanda LeClere
Author Photo by Devin Harkness.
Design by Jason Schneiderman

Pleasure Boat Studio books are available through the following:
SPD (Small Press Distribution) Tel. 800-869-7553, Fax 510-524-0852
Partners/West Tel. 425-227-8486, Fax 425-204-2448
Baker & Taylor 800-775-1100, Fax 800-775-7480
Ingram Tel 615-793-5000, Fax 615-287-5429
Amazon.com and bn.com and through

PLEASURE BOAT STUDIO: A LITERARY PRESS
www.pleasureboatstudio.com
201 West 89th Street
New York, NY 10024

Contact Jack Estes
Fax; 888-810-5308
Email: pleasboat@nyc.rr.com

ACKNOWLEDGEMENTS

Between the Lines: "Tracks in Snow"

Crosscurrents: "1965"

Fine Madness: "Lao Wang," "Star Chart Goes Missing," "Dead Chinook, North Fork"

Great River Review: "Telescope in the Basement," "Beautiful Passing Lives"

The Humanist: "Against Optimism"

The Louisville Review: "Aunt Bea's Trailer"

Midwest Quarterly: "Rattlesnake Creek, South Fork,"

Poets Against the War (online): "The Day the War Began"

The Salt River Review (online): "One Less Fall," "Out of the Blue"

Spindrift: "Rattlesnake Creek: After the Flood," "Mountain Ash Berries,"

"Abandoned Igloo," "Nelson Bentley Alone in Savery Hall," "Tour of Kilmainham Gaol," "Elaboration on a Statement by Frost"

Square Lake #1: "Crazy Snow"

Switched-on Gutenberg (online): "Second Bull Run," "Why We Hike to the Duck Marsh"

The following poems first appeared in *Syringa in Twilight*, a chapbook, published by Red Wing Press, 2010: "Jock Itch," "Syringa in Twilight," "Unfinished Cabin Above the Creek"

TABLE OF CONTENTS

For Linda, and for Devin and Ned

Rattlesnake Creek

Wind, bird, and tree,
Water, grass, and light:
In half of what I write
Roughly or smoothly
Year by impatient year,
The same six words recur.
—David Wagoner

AFTER THE FLOOD

This would be the spot where last August
a dozen chinooks shook their beaten bodies.
The shallows where they spawned
got taken out along with half the trees.
All that's left is a stretch of sun-hot gravel,
tumbled in channels and mounds.

Tame and silted green from the May runoff,
the creek glides closer to the highway now,
High water gouged the bank below the guardrail.
Stumps lie where they fell. A ponderosas pine
must have careened through the gorge
Its ragged roots implore an impassive sky.

Even the north fork bridge collapsed,
rebar and concrete blocks bouncing for miles,
then settled here like Roman ruins.
A raccoon left a sentence in the muck.
You can see why Leonardo sketched water
hour after hour, sluicing over stones—

the curls, the whorls. In a bed of cobbles,
a bouquet has forced its way to the light,
the trumpet of each flower blaring red.
Just when a landscape looks most wasted,
and your memory erased along with it, is the moment
you kneel and discover a flower called foxfire.

North Fork

First one I've seen this far up the canyon.
Creek boulders have banged my shins raw.
I've fallen only twice. Lost my cap and bird book.
Now it's just me and this dead chinook,
eyeless on the rocks, side chewed by raccoons
to reveal the curved white needles of ribs.

This is it, what I was meant to come across—
the old metaphor for migratory cycles,
upstream journeys. Tiny yellow flowers
eke out a living in the basalt, so hardy,
so delicate, I want to remember them
as paint spattered on a dungeon wall.

On the return, there's the salmon again,
still dead, still examining my motives
for wading all this way.
I strip, step into a pool and take the plunge.
When I rocket up, I shout my explanation—
the first guttural words of a new tongue.

Tracks in Snow

Bear, maybe, or, more likely, elk.
A day old at least, they wandered riverward,
blurred by last night's fall.

Smoke ribbons from the cabin chimney.
Cottonwood. Sweetness gave it away.
At the sound of snow crunch,

I turned and—wonder of wonders—
you stood in your blue parka,
tracking me to the gravel bar.

Those other tracks were mine, of course,
made the day before. I'd paused
by a wild rose, each hard hip

snow-specked, and remembered
their pink pungency in the heat of July.
Karma, call it. Call it one of those things.

It's not the first time I've covered
the same ground, looping back
to a starting point under spidery aspens,

back to words I can't let go of:
aspen, rose, river, snow, and,
wonder of wonders, *you,*

my blue guide, my traveling companion,
wrapped in the rasp of the river,
the snow crunch, by the rose.

South Fork

It takes half a day of wading to find
the deep eddies. Even in August heat
the current hurts. The creek does a better job
than me at accepting my aging face.

When I leap in, I know I'm a man.
It's the punch of a heart attack. Explosive.
I open my eyes to a storm of bubbles,
bits of wood and colored stones.

It has taken most of my life to get here.
I clamber onto the sand
and shake off the good pain.
The scent of pines is all I need
to love the world again.

Unfinished Cabin Above the Creek

There's no sweeter view of water and stone.
The creek tumbles down from Elk Ridge to here,
a ledge where the cabin stands, vacant as air
passing through the missing door, windows open
to swallows or snow. A family of bats must live
in the half-built river-rock chimney.

The top logs are newer peeled pine, still tan,
knots like eyes of deer lost in the wood.
I'd say they've watched the ridge for twenty years.
The lower courses look older, darker,
split in places, though still sound, black gaps
where chunks of bone white mortar have fallen out.

At ground level, gray foundation logs list a bit,
out of true, in slow collapse back to dirt.
They must have been laid in the '40s—
someone's dream place the dreamer returned to
now and then for fun, for the creek smell,
the good ache of his arms after a day's work.

Maybe the dreamer didn't care what completion meant,
a summer here and there, the dreamer losing sight
of what the dream might give: ridgeline, star track,
wood smoke, hummingbird, heron, hawk.
Or—Who knows?—the dreamer tired and moved on,
married, divorced, or lost the need for solitude.

Or died. The dreamer got this far and stopped.
No regrets. Who can say the cabin isn't done?
Inside its useless walls, three seedling pines
climb toward light from the dreamer's rotted floor.
He'll never know his children. They're at home
in his dream, in a world that goes on without him.

Out of the Blue

Now and then it happens,
often in March, the sun
a dazzle in the bare aspens.

Blown from clouds
hidden behind Bethel Ridge,
snow will fall out of the blue

like sparks, a swarm of glitter,
floating first as feathers,
then cool specks on your cheek,

like tears from far away.
One moment,
you're listing all your failings.

The next, you're standing with your lover
on a gravel bar,
showered in a confetti of light.

Aunt Bea's Trailer

"Writing is a way of saying you and the world have
a chance. All art is failure."
—Richard Hugo

Final Tryout This Saturday Noon

That was the day he knew he'd never fit in,
Sunday, church just out across the park,
blossoms on the ornamental cherries
pink as a Buick convertible in the sunny lot.
He had his father's glove, his gray splintery bat,
handle wrapped with electrical tape,
and there he stood at third, alone on the diamond,
the only other soul a hunched woman in a shawl
tossing bread to geese in weedy left field.

The line of elms beyond the backstop filled
with wind and the wind said Kid, give it up.
You're one day behind in your life,
miles from home, Dad not due back till dusk.
Maybe never due back. Give it up, kid.
Your sneakers are dumb as dirt.

He felt like the water fountain. Broken.
No cap, no coat, four hours to shiver and play ball
in his head, winning the game on a triple,
the coach beaming, cheers from every neighbor.
After the long walk home he was glad no one
at the dinner table asked. If they'd asked,
he'd have said the nice coach gave him a lift,
he'd made the team, he'd be playing third.

THE LAKEVIEW WEEKLY NEIGHBOR

He'd ride in the January chill
before school, the canvas bag
slapping his knees on the up crank
to the green shed where the papers

waited in their bundles. He'd load
the bag front and back, glide past
the Lakeview Methodist Church,
its lone stained glass window

obscured by a billboard for Shell Oil.
He'd round a corner to Bud's Meats,
glimpse Bud through a side door,
in his bloody apron, cutting steaks.

The last few stars would close their eyes.
He'd enter dark tunnels of cedars,
coast down a drive toward the lake
as far as he dared, skid in the gravel,

dismount, fold a paper and huck it
high over a fence or laurel hedge
toward a porch light. He'd watch the paper
spin end over end, then pivot and pedal,

gravel crunching under his wheels.
That's when his heart banged loudest,
steeled for the Doberman or Labrador
he knew lay waiting in the trees.

Back at the pavement,
he'd pause for a ten-count,
thrilled by the streetlight on Densmore,
convinced more than ever

he wasn't cut out for this. He'd heard
of something called the afterlife.
As he coasted, wobbled and picked up speed,
he wondered if this was it.

Tangerines in L.A.

How did we manage to clear the barbed wire?
Even in moonlight, we could see the house
was vacant, tall grass like wild silver hair.

I'd never seen spears of eucalyptus,
or felt heavy heat at midnight,
or heard crickets that loud, as if someone

in the orchard was scraping bricks in the dark.
Low limbs jabbed my cheek. Here they are,
my cousin said. They hung like black apples,

casting oval shadows on the ground.
Many had fallen. When we stepped on them
they burst and sighed, sweetening the night air

with their acids. My cousin threw one at me.
Bits of tangerine slid down my bare calf,
wetting my socks. I was thirteen,
beside myself with homesickness.

I knew this night would one day return
in some vague future I could not imagine,
like a postcard from an invented world.
I snatched handfuls of tangerines,

ripped them in half, juice stinging my eyes.
I shoved chunks in my mouth,
peeling and all, gagging on their ripeness,
their sweetness, their tang.

1965

While she shopped, he sat sullen in the car,
pushing the stupid buttons on the radio,
passed news of Vietnam, our newest war.

He'd flipped his physics book in the back,
its pages of laws and equations
a black hole he'd never fathom.

Waves of July heat pulsed off the asphalt.
He pictured a melting world: stores,
people, his high school, the hospital

where he empties bedpans on weekends—
all the things that made him wonder
what the hell he was doing with his

time on earth. He punched another button.
Odd silence. Dead air. Then, bam!
the snap of a snare drum slapped him.

Once upon a time you dressed so fine /
You threw the bums a dime
in your prime, didn't you?

He barely heard the words
but heard them. He cranked the volume
till the one speaker sizzled in its metal grille.

For the next six minutes
he understood the universe.
He'd later learn the passionate

scratchy whine was Dylan's,
but now, sunlight made sense.
The gray Oldsmobile rolled on waves

of sound. He'd fail physics, but that
didn't matter. Someone out there
knew what everything meant.

CRAZY SNOW

The night uncle Charles died he asked Miriam, his second wife, to bring a photograph of Larry, Charles' son, killed in Viet Nam, July of '68. She finds a shot of Larry taken not six months before his death. It's a winter scene. Larry's on skis, rose-cheeked, smart-aleck grin, goggles on his forehead, his purple parka dotted with snow. His eyes are dark. A three day growth of beard stains his face. He's engaged to a girl named Clare. They plan to marry in a meadow above Lake Tahoe. We get a call one warm night from Clare, her voice a whisper, saying Larry's dead, far away, no details. Thirty years pass like thirty years. My uncle, dying, believes by gazing at the picture of his boy he'll close his eyes, open them, and there Larry will be, grinning, ready for a final run before dark sets in, and Uncle Charles says Let me take one more to remember you by. Charles knows his boy will die, but he can't bring himself to reveal this—It's his boy, his only boy. Snow needles Charles' gloveless hands. The place is Heavenly Valley, a few miles above Tahoe. Eight inches of new powder have fallen. Father and son stand together by the chairlift floodlit in a blue ring of neon, snow sparking about them, the picture now face down on Charles' chest, his eyes open, his lips working to say Larry, don't go. One more shot, just one. I can't see you in this crazy snow.

VIETNAM

I blamed them for his death. They weren't to blame.
The country was. They bought the country's lies.
Someone carved his name on the wall of time.

A midnight call. A voice from far away
saying he's gone, he's gone, too late for goodbyes.
I blamed them for his death. They weren't to blame.

History is a deep and twisted cave.
We hide our handprints from wondering eyes.
Someone carved his name on the wall of time

where other names whisper night and day
About the lives they never had—all *ifs*, no *whys*.
I blamed them for his death. They weren't to blame—

nor was I, who said *No* to the killing game,
No to lessons all boys and girls learn to prize.
Someone carved his name on the wall of time.

His name remembers the hike to an alpine lake.
Loons wounded the evening air with their cries.
I blame the loons for his death. They're not to blame.
Someone carved his name on the wall of time.

Charlotte Harkness, July 1876

Two of your boys died in four days,
Bobby and George. That was Iowa,
where corn rolled in on green tides.
Charlotte, what's a mother to do?
You buried them in Graceland, Hardin County,
and there, in 1904, they laid you down
beside them and your husband, Robert,
near your other little ones, Esther and Ruth.

Only David survived, outlived you by a year
before he fell, uncoupling cars in the rail yard,
leaving Bertha and his boys in Estherville.
I'm twice his twenty nine. Made it by a corn silk thread,
you might have said had you not been,
as the census taker wrote, "deaf and dumb."
Someone needs to clear the weeds.
They choke the dead.

A hundred summers have broken your stones.
I want to ask them what it takes for wind
to lift us over the line of elms, above the squares
of winter wheat. You must have wondered too,
those August evenings, watching David sleep,
unable to hear the ebb and flow of his breath,
thinking of all those jars of plums,
and no one to eat them but him.

Aunt Bea's Trailer

The job of the living is to clean up—
fill cardboard boxes, haul them to Goodwill,
pause before taking on the refrigerator
to read the wall calendar with its penciled squares:
Jul. 14: Hysterectomy
Jul. 18: Pay bills
Jul. 29: Salmon fishing, LaPush, w/ Marshall
Then pull out the thumbtack
and drop a year into the garbage bag.
I still have the neon Sears hunter's cap with ear flaps
the one she bought for my move to Montana,
convinced as she was I'd die of cold or be shot.

The job of the living is to take note:
cribbage board, gardening gloves,
green glass earrings—all casual on the end table,
their final resting place by the 12-inch color TV.

Three marriages, no kids. Now what to do
with the shoe box of birthday cards and photos.
A recent one shows her on the tiny couch
with Max, her terrier. She's a little heavy,
still pretty to me, her silver hair in 1940's waves.
That's the Avery grin, a hint of the wicked,
the reason I was drawn to her most of all.

In this crinkled black and white she's no older
than 14, plaid skirt, gray blouse, pushing a bike
on a gravel road, beach in the background.
A breeze sweeps the skirt forward, her hair too,
hiding a coy eye. Her legs are lithe and long.
Same Avery grin. Her left foot pauses on the pedal,
poised to push off and coast into the life
she has coming. Then there's the suitcase of letters

from a man in Maine. Years of them. Weekly.
She'd hidden them in an upper closet shelf.
They have to wait for the day I can sit down
and enter a side door to her inner world.
The suitcase and these two pictures I keep.
Everything else must go, as it always has.

Boiling a Watch

"If people around you are in favor, that helps poetry to **be**, to exist. It disappears under disfavor. There are things, you know, human things, that depend on commitment; poetry is one of those things. If you analyze it away, it's gone. It would be like boiling a watch to find out what makes it tick."
—William Stafford

Stunning, He Thought that Morning,

the sun just risen, igniting the lilac peaks
as he crossed the pass, his flatbed
loaded with its tarped cargo.

Then the two-hour descent to the city.
He hadn't factored in rush-hour.
It slowed his arrival at the place he hated.
What the campus guards at the gate

said to him, or what they thought
of the truck, the man, can't be known.
Classes had just let out.
Students gathered on the lawn

by the main campus road, there to attend
a vigil for the Mi Lai dead.
A Buddhist monk in yellow robe chanted—
the only sound other than wild arias

of robins in the leafing trees.
Someone had passed out daffodils.
The driver saw three hundred traitors.
He pulled to the curb unobserved,

his head in its wire mesh cage.
Four hundred now, he guessed,
more strolling in. He untied the ropes.
Incense drifted over the bowed heads.

When he pulled the tarp, a gold cloud
of honeybees exploded from the white hives,
then descended roaring in the air.
People screamed as he threw the truck in gear.

He saw them run and stumble and writhe
in his rearview mirror. When he crossed
the pass, ice on the peaks flared
in midday sun. Stunning.

A Rusted Piece of German Barbed Wire

It's a robin's foot, so fragile I could
crush it with a pinch and ruin history.
Omaha sand is red, as if to remind me
of the landing. The Channel looks benign,
a road of hammered silver. Unglamorous,
windswept, this beach is no Riviera.
Here you feel the slap of the beyond.

What's beyond could be beautiful.
What's here would never work as a movie—
way too flat for dramatic camera angles.
No bluffs for Rangers to scale or Germans
to enfilade from above. Still, this is where
boys drowned or fell after a couple of steps
in quickening sand, day just breaking.
A mile south B-24s bombed bunkers into blocks
the size of trucks. They stick out of the grass
like the corners of a buried city.

We drive to the American cemetery
to see an eternity of crosses—
Italian marble and laid out with such precision
everything else is chaos, senseless.
James Clay, 19, Ohio. Endless garden of names.

The red claw in my hand might have snared
one of them. I pried it out of a jeep track
above high tide. Big revelation: iron rusts.
Back at the beach wind has kicked up whitecaps.
A kid flies a kite. In a pasture with a sweeping view,
cows graze, and the day passes as if to say
nothing this bad could have happened. No storms,
no wars, just a beach and the lulling waves.

German Man on the Train to Munich

He's eighty, dapper still in his gray suit.
English good, eyes clear, a smile not quite right.
Yes, he fought in the war, wounded four times,
each time patched and sent back to face Russians
coming this way, GIs that. And Hitler?
"Ach, a common thug." He says "thug,"
and it sounds rehearsed, easy. Eighty years,
his chin still quivers when he remembers,
as if there are decades he can't accept,
a history no one understands but him.
No mention of the Jews. He lifts his hands–
two fingers on one, three on the other.
"Grenades," he says. "They went off early, twice."
He became a radiologist, now retired.
He praises German cars—he himself just bought
a new Mercedes–"Finest auto in the world,
I think, yes?" He tells us what to see in Munich,
where to find the best German beer.
On the station platform he bows goodbye.

We stroll the grounds of Dachau, through barracks
where prisoners slept naked on slats.
I picture coils of acrid smoke roiling
from chimneys above the ovens burning
round the clock. I see his German smile.
Here, half a million rose as ash. The ash
fell back each day for years on inmates, on guards,
on houses in nearby towns, their gardens, their ponds.
That ash dusted kids dawdling to school
in June, tainted snow at Christmas—
a stain no one could miss. When we leave,
the dead remain, still starving, still chained.
They're everywhere—underfoot, in the lungs

of local elders, in the bark of older elms.
Some of the ash may have risen high enough.
Some of the ash may have made it to the clouds.

CAR CAMPING IN THE OZARKS

We could hear them in the dark across the lake
scream at their children,
If you make one more sound,
by God, I'll give ya something to cry about.

That was the mother. Stars hung over the water
like a bracelet broken, flung and frozen
in the blue black. Then more crying,
then a man—perhaps the father—swore.

Their huge fire illumined a tent, a white van
and their orange wavering faces.
Then cackling from mother and father,
then whoops from several others.

We could see the glow of their cigarettes.
We heard splashes from tossed empties,
crackle of the fire. At the lake's far end,
frogs sang to the enduring world.

Then we heard a girl's cry. A woman growled
Go on, ya baby. It ain't that dark.
Small waves washed the gravel.
We wondered how it was we could listen

and do nothing, fearful of the Missouri night,
afraid of what we knew was in that van.
We sat mute, unable to face the bullies,
unable to rise up to tyrants and say stop.

Second Bull Run

Sunlight dapples the maples. My park map says
this is where the skirmish occurred near
the slanted cabin, its dovetail joints still firm.
Weather has knocked loose clay mortar from the logs.
The windows are black, out of square, unreadable,
glaring these odd hundred thirty years
since children climbed peach trees off the porch.
That was before the first cracks of musket fire,
before dust of ten thousand horses
rose and settled over the valley, August, 1862.

Where did the family flee when they heard
the clank of caissons on the road,
the teamsters cursing? What did they think
as they watched regimental pennants whip and snap?
Bees droned on the fermented ground
where acres of dusty peaches fell.

A Park Service marker says *You Are Here.*
A split rail fence once looped across this bare
grassy rise. The marker displays a passage
encased in a plastic window someone has defaced
with a stone, half-erasing a page from a vet's diary.
He would have stood behind the rails that afternoon
loading and firing, faint with thirst. He recalled
he heard the thump of bullets hitting boys
crouched nearby. Many wailed. Some laughed.
The fence, they thought, kept them hidden.
He writes he never felt pain when wood splinters
raked his cheek. To his left a fellow he knew as Will gasped,
turned and said *Oh lordy, I'm a dead man,*
then sagged, the vet remembered, *like a sack of meal.*

The grass path to the parking lot shows hardly any wear.
Even before I get to my car, I'm writing my own diary,
wondering how to describe the gentle hills.

Capture of a Confederate Soldier

His horse leapt and snorted at the snap
of the distant rifle report just as he felt
the yank on his dirty gray pants
where the bullet tore through the cloth.
He knew he wasn't going to die, but damn
it hurt, as if someone had taken a hammer
to his thigh, and it burned too—
he caught a whiff of his own charred meat.
He dismounted and sat hard in the mud
outside of Nashville. He was 44,
still had most of his teeth, a wild beard
showing the first touch of silver.
The war was over, as far as he was concerned,
his part, surely. His thigh began to throb.
Blood mixed with the slop he'd landed in.
His mind was clear, hawk-like,
taking in the scene from far above.
He could see the pine forest,
the pale road winding through it,
a white church on the bank of a creek,
and a half dozen blue coats
approaching on their skittish horses,
surrounding a tiny figure he understood
was himself, defeated and wounded.
He saw too his farm in Kentucky—
his wife tending the garden, one of the boys
switching a cow across a field,
an elder daughter skinning a rabbit.
He signed on late for reasons he couldn't explain—
defending the South, whatever that meant.
They were shouting at him, the Yankees,
their Spensers raised and cocked.
He couldn't hear what they were saying.
He lay back and stretched out his arms.

The mud, he noticed, was warm.
Even the flies didn't bother him.
He'd live through this, neither proud nor ashamed.
He'd been born, after all, a Virginian.
Rightness would be for others to consider.
Maybe there'd come a time
when men wouldn't shoot each other.
He'd be dust by then. But lying in the muck
and horse shit, his thigh hot with swelling,
seven rifles pointed at his head,
he hoped that day would come.

AGAINST OPTIMISM

It's a lonely fight, no more so than when
the broken rhododendron—a decrepit
mass of twisted limbs just off the back porch—
flares for two fiery weeks each May,
so scarlet and profuse, so labial
it rattles me. I'm filled with doubt.

I email a friend about the dark we swim in,
a triumph complete and incontrovertible.
Any sharp 9th grader can see it.
My friend writes back, sings the hymn of religion,
demands I give equal billing to the bright side
and signs off, "Dripping with optimism."

Look, it's the 11th century, I'm a monk,
I go my solitary way, believing not so much
that the end is nigh but that the end happened
when we were children and still viewed the world
as a marvelous peach. It was a brief dream.
We hadn't learned yet that cheerful men

develop weapons systems. Then one day,
spading the potato patch, I dig up a cateye marble.
I wipe away the crumbs of earth and marvel
at its green iris, luminous after all those years
underground. A kid must have dropped it,
a girl, I suppose, whose family built our house

around the time of the Great Depression.
I suppose it would have been her mother
who planted the back porch rhody,
the wild gnarled thing in full flower,
shrieking, almost, with magenta, the one
I've stared at now for the better part of an hour.

The Day the War Began

I split a few pine rounds,
stacked them between a pair
of small just-yellowing aspens.

Chickadees chattered in a bare
elderberry limb. For an hour
the tang of cut pine

lingered in the evening air.
I changed the well pump filter.
In the failing light

I followed elk tracks—
a bull, cow and calf—
down the needle-strewn trail

to the river, their prints
deep in the mud along the shore.
Somehow I had missed them

as they browsed noiselessly
in a stand of cottonwoods
before they entered the current.

I was aware of nothing
but the wild smell of roses,
the river inhaling so faintly

I could hear my heart whisper
over and over: *not again
not again not again.*

Boiling a Watch

My hope: to see the steam of time rise,
clouding my glasses. What might happen
if I'm blinded by the mist where history hides?

Or if I inhale too deeply the vapor of minutes
and centuries? Those must be Hitler's reading glasses,
there are Napoleon's blood-specked boots,

and now blocks of a pyramid glide away,
pulling elephants back to the quarry,
leaving the lone sands monumentally bare,

flooded now by the warm first ocean,
frothy with lime green swells.
The watch simmers in its pot of hours,

ticking, stretched like taffy, a dripping
Dali painting, the brown leather wristband
wrinkled in broth clear as original arctic air.

I ladle it into a white bowl, garnished
with roman numerals. The second hand
floats to the surface, bobbing like a tiny oar.

Time is more fluid than I thought,
flavored with the salt of now, and like a poem,
tasting of everything that ever happened.

The Scar on Yeats' Cheek

CAN MURDERERS LEAD SUCCESSFUL LIVES?

Happily, yes. They too admire
the small green knives of summer grass.
They enjoy brisk walks like we do.
They love the sweetness of rain rinsed air
singing in their lungs.

They too love the flutter and whisper
of bamboo. They have families,
and care about the schools
where their children learn the ABCs
and vie for roles in the spring play.

Do murderers feel sorrow? Of course—
especially when the dead are far away.
Killing may not even occur
to murderers for quiet country roads
of their lives, as when in childhood they

collected beetles or mastered the unicycle
or, later, studied anatomy for artists,
and later still, ran a winning senate campaign.
The lives of murderers occupy
many library shelves, blessed by

the gold dust of time, and though
murderers die as we all must, often
they outlive us, have grandchildren
and great-grandchildren, who will
follow the family line

to much applause, much gratitude, even,
from coalitions of the murderer's friends.

Let's lay to rest the myth of murderer
as repulsive beast couched in our shrubs
or slashing the throats of newspapers.

That's the movie version.
Murderers often come from the better families,
the ones who own the thought refineries.
Despite their fame, their prominence in the pews,
the best murderers can't be identified

let alone caught. Why? Witnesses refused
to testify. Thus, nothing happened.
The bodies were taken away at night,
flown to lands owned by friends of the murderer.
There, ravens ate them—men, women, children,

all the same. And since the evidence wheels
in and out of clouds, out of sight like truth, like horror,
it's safe to stroll barefoot the moonlit beach,
hear small waves break the silence, feel cool sand
between our toes just like the murderers.

FIVE ANGRY LITTLE SONGS

1.

Boil me in oil, Lord. I've inhaled bad air
blurred with the chain store smoke of death.
I bought into the American Scream. I swear
I'll go psycho if I take one more breath.

My pastor says he'll kill me if I lie to God.
I see cities desolate as a mayor's brain,
rivers of mute survivors trudge on sod
turned to sand after the swan song of rain.

We used to discuss nature. Now the topic is ice.
For our purposes, let ice stand for loss,
let loss stand for whatever you think is nice,
let nice stand for the velvety memory of moss.

Our lifestyle choice is suicidal.
Everyone's into it. Not one hand is idle.

2.

The daily news IEDs my brain.
Reporters upchuck the king's every ivory word,
and I quote: "The sea are a airy barren plain."
The king is drunk with certainty, his words are slurred.

Snow and cancer fog, acid sun and rain—
It's another icy July. On Fox I heard a herd
of rhinos trampled the king's roses. Please explain,
oh king. Forget cognition. We need to be reassured

we own the earth by right of godly domain.
The castle correspondents have conferred
with the cast, warned them not to complain
about our present pall. Some cancers can't be cured.

The lies, America. The king pissed on our name.
We're terminal. The king! The king's to blame!

3.

I suppose it's my fault I stumbled here
where lilacs ignite when you touch their skin.
It's not what I expected—all this fear,
all these means of torture, and not one a sin.

The Dark Ages has its ups and downs.
I saw a man drawn and quartered. Some laughed
at the gush of blood, the ghastly sounds.
I noted every detail. Noting is my craft.

I'm an expert witness. I record horror
in the hope that others will recoil at the sight.
We chose hell, and for that we're the poorer.
They literally burn time here day and night.

It's the groaning I hate, my own groaning.
Speaking in tongues is my way of atoning.

4.

Bernardo my 'bro, it's a rotten world.
Let's bomb the shit out of everything.
We're number one! This flag is God unfurled,
and when it flies, buddy, you'd better sing.

Bernardo, Denmark's fine—it's your countrymen
I fear. All that righteous ignorance
has turned the land into a thieves' den.
The king kills, then claims his innocence.

Tonight the moon aims its high beams
on bones strewn across an Iraqi plain.
We did this. I saw a family's dreams
shot dead at a checkpoint—every member slain.

Denmark decayed, Bernardo, while you slept.
If Hamlet had lived, he would have wept.

5.

It takes an afternoon to pound her hair
into iron. It's a helmet she requires.
She offers her wisdom, her granite stare
of rightness. Her cool words ignite fires.

She tells the king she loves half the truth,
He's good with that. Her diamond brilliance
must not be questioned. It would be uncouth
if the war this pair cooked up made sense.

Reporters adore her. They kiss her feet
without being ordered, then crawl away.
When kids are cut down like wheat
by cluster bombs, she has nothing to say.

She's the king's councilor, maybe more,
maybe co-defendant, big star, hardcore.

Falling Asleep Next to My Fountain Pen

Someone has murdered my sheets. That blue blood
was supposed to be lines about a bowl of plums.

If I could have stayed awake,
you'd be listening to music almost as good as Bach

or Mississippi John Hurt singing "Sliding Delta."
Instead, I slid under the dark waves of sleep

to find myself tiptoeing down a road paved
with raisins. There's my father as a teenager

waving in a field of cornflakes in Hardin County, Iowa.
If I'd stayed awake, you'd hear a far truer account

of my private life, a confession about a bad thing I did.
I'd have a transcript of all my arguments

on behalf of lost causes. What I recall is dampness,
a distant seepage, a wound with no location.

It was Lady Macbeth whose mind cracked
in the vise of a crime. Some stains are forever,

she understood, like these inky storm clouds.
They are my indecipherable epitaph,

everything I never wrote, a wet dream only darker,
more permanent, a testament to lost art everywhere.

Star Chart Goes Missing

It's supposed to be on the bookshelf,
sandwiched between Rilke and Roethke.

Above the black teeth of trees
stars begin their show

joined by three bats writing in Arabic
in the deep paper of the sky.

I try to recall the names of princesses,
warriors, serpents and winged horses,

then search for flecks of light
shaped supposedly like a goat.

I lean back in a folding chair
and study instead a candle flame

blinking in an attic window
of a darkened nearby farmhouse.

And I wonder who lives there,
what might she be writing at this hour.

Now I see it's not a candle but Sirius,
the Dog Star, lifting its drowsy head,

guarding the dog house of heaven
with its one yellow eye.

THE PRESENT

The lake of memory shines
on summer afternoons.
What's in it holds to the bottom,
attached as lilies are to the soft

vague silt by long cables
rising toward the light.
They climb to the still surface—
green raft, yellow survivor.

On the far shore, small voices
carry across the stillness—
splashes of talk,
children's inaudible cries.

The past is a murky thing.
Some remnants will bob up,
even after years, connected
to the hidden earth.

Others, however,
we will never see again.
As for the present,
those faint voices we hear

come from our lost selves,
alive forever in the light of late July.
The lake is who we are—
seen and unseen and deep.

To the Future

You're wrong about us.
We were not the barbarians you imagine.
Look, we came up with arrow points,

bricks, the plow. We gave you paper,
bar codes. But you've decided we were
crude souls because we defended ourselves

against the forces of horror
or read the mind of our Maker
in spiders' webs. We destroyed

what we had to destroy, and were in turn
cursed with plagues unleashed by those
who played off our fear of the sky.

You sneer now, but we prevailed,
though it meant taking drastic steps
with the skin of those

whose prayers and dances
were incompatible with our own,
not to mention the squawk

they called their mother tongue.
Like you, we worshipped roses.
We too refused to let our children

see that psycho-clown, the moon,
disfigured by ancient sins.
We gave you the tools

to travel with light,
to bring star tracks to your front door.
Do not think, however,

that we were of one mind,
that we all believed the prince.
Many were sick unto death

inside the tortured climate
he designed, made mad by the murders
he committed each time he pursed his lips.

Look into your heart's data recovery system.
Imagine us as kin, as blood,
not distant at all but in fact near as breath.

We loved our children to pieces
but gave them away sometimes
to those who saw a higher purpose,

and it hurt, as it always does,
to say goodbye
to those pure trusting eyes.

Our greatest failing: we couldn't raise
the dead, not in any convincing way.
Perhaps you have puzzled

this out by entering our tombs,
hacking our hidden files
from the sectors of silence.

You are wrong, I suppose,
as we may have been wrong about our cousins
who lived before, whose odd stares

posed a grave threat. Evil
can be recycled like everything,
as you now know.

We only wanted to disperse.
Surely your ornate stems hum to this pulse.
Not all, perhaps,

but the horde of you—the majority—
have gone remote control,
ignorant of our sacrifices

that interfaced with your survival.
That would include our celestials—
remember Jeanne, remember Rachel.

And from where you crouch
or sail or stream through the gold canals
of your shadeless world,

consider how history works:
the future's future
will be wrong about you.

The Language of the Dead

The hard part is translating their shadowy tongue,
earlier even than Latin. They converse sometimes
in bursts of urgency, sometimes telepathically,

as if phoning from a sunken liner.
They never plead but they do insist, the gist being:
We're at peace on this side despite the monotony

of darkness so perpetual it is the absence of absence.
The dead may be a race of blind prisoners
unable to feel the walls that contain them.

What do they mean when they liken lilacs to eons?
Or war to the warble of paper? Rarely do they appear
shrouded in vapor as countless tales claim.

Their voices, though, often float nearby not as groans
or threats but as melancholy improvisations
from their fog-filled hearts. Days or years later

we might remember the words they transmitted,
the sweet right words, and realize no one knows us
better than they. No one sympathizes more

with what it's like to walk the earth. They speak
from experience. They peer into our living eyes
even though to them we are transparent, like ghosts.

ELABORATION ON A STATEMENT BY FROST

A poem begins in delight and ends in wisdom.

A poem begins around 4:40 on the afternoon of April 19.
Hard to say where it's going—whether to the market
of ears and eyes or to Emperor Qin's underground kingdom—
or if it has plans to sit in the sunlight and read itself.
It begins, despite having to stand unblindfolded
before the firing squad of the Friends of Poetry,
in delight, even though all is lost. In traveling from heart
to heart, it might beat or enter a death-like state
or break into salty song, as sailors do when they spy Gibraltar.
A poem ends, in most cases. Those that don't end
are still out there in the desert, searching for water.
A poem that does end, could possibly end in wisdom
or in jail, or in Nova Scotia. If it ends in wisdom,
count yourself lucky. You don't have to go to jail
to read the poem. You don't have to go to Nova Scotia.

THE SCAR ON YEATS' CHEEK

In the photo it's a long thin smile
on the left side, winding like a road map
upward from his upper lip.
Under a magnifying glass, a Martian canyon
travels the desert of his face.
His hair is mussed, the sideburns
neatly squared below the top of his ear.
His reading glasses rest on his young nose,
a gold chain dangling from the right lens.
The bow tie looks extravagant, knotted
gift-like against the high white collar
haloing his throat—hardly the image
of a pub brawler. The camera has framed
his head in half profile,
so he seems not twenty five but twice that,
at least around the black opals of his eyes.
They gaze downward to the left—intent,
resigned, not sad but rather steeled as if
committed to a life of watchfulness.
He could be looking at a tripod
propped in a corner of the studio,
or a cat curled on a windowsill.
He could be musing about Maude Gonne,
the dark flag of her hair, or the Rising
still decades away, so the scar would be
a preview of "Easter 1916"
scrawled jaggedly up his clean-shaved cheek.
Or he's thinking about lunch or his own hair,
a few wild locks tumbled on his forehead
so that the viewer will know he's a poet
peering forever into the deep pool
of what has been and what's to come.
His face is his signature. He's a marked man,
and the proof would be that scar.

Telescope in the Basement

"I have been trusting another sort of
communication between you and me—a sort
of message from the heart—sent by thinking of
you and feeling great love for you and knowing
strongly that you think of me, that you are sending
thoughts and feelings to me; and you and I, Jim,
we *trust* in these message that move between us."
—Leslie Marmon Silko

NELSON BENTLEY SITTING ALONE IN SAVERY HALL

He was too forgiving, as angels usually are.
Squat, balding Buddha in plaid shirt, sleeves
rolled to the elbow, his W.C. Fields impersonation
was funnier than Fields. He had Ariel's pearly eyes,
full of pure sprite. For decades he led us on,
hosted weekly student readings here in dusty Savery,
never to more than a dozen listeners hunched
on the tiered wood benches, the hall's beige linoleum
worn thin at the door where slow rivers of freshmen
entered and suffered lectures on Kierkegaard or Milton.

Those Wednesday afternoons we got to rise
to the lectern. He'd introduce the three readers,
then sit to the side in a folding chair while we went at it
in mumbles, whispers and inexplicable shouts,
our names chalked large on the board behind
in Nelson's immaculate capitals. Who knows why
he loved us or why he laughed when we cracked wise
in a poem. Tess read. So did Laura and Jim
and Paul—a few who shone in poetry's little glade.
Others peeled away like the paint on the Savery walls.

I'm early. Already Nelson has chalked the names.
Oh Jesus, one is mine. Gnomic, slovenly, a slouched
hermit of devotion, he fumbles with his drugstore
note pad, a stub of yellow pencil in his thick fingers,
rehearsing the good things he plans to say about us,
noting the unknown journals that might
or might not have published something of ours.
I'm light-headed with stage fright, praying no one shows
and we'll have to cancel. But the two other readers
arrive with their three friends. When Nelson calls on me
I float up with my sheaf of poems and for ten deadly minutes
I mutter. That's what he gave us: the chance to mutter.

Also: patience, the steady heart of kindness you encounter
in a person, and it takes forty years before it registers.

What I did not learn—from him or anyone—
was the sitting, the waiting, poetry's long haul,
where you wonder if anyone will show, or why,
hoping they don't so you can go home and stash
your little secrets back in the cardboard box—
hoping they do so you can rise to the lectern
and face five or six invisible listeners,
and hear Nelson, your champion, off to the side,
chuckle at some little joke in your poem.

Tour of Kilmainham Gaol

We stand where the Easter Risers fell
and sprawled on the yard's trampled grass.
British bullets left those pocks in the granite,
about chest level. The Irishmen wore blindfolds.

The central cell ceiling is stained glass—
not God's colors, exactly; stained rather
by centuries of crows and coal. Given light,
enlightened prison designers believed,

men's eyes would rise toward heaven, goodness,
reform. As we know, it never happened.
When prisoners lifted their gaze, they saw soot
streaked by rain into eternal winter evening.

Notice the smell of mildew in the cells.
Dampness was a Kilmainham fact of life.
Eighty years ago the prison closed, the last inmate
released to actual daylight and his thoughts.

Perhaps he saw history as a prison full of promise,
held captive by the wisdom of the times,
most of it nonsense. He might have asked why it is
we kill for flags and ideas and feel right.

Some who know the poem "Easter 1916" will recall
the name of Connolly. He'd been wounded earlier
and so was offered a chair. When soldiers fired,
the ceiling glass rattled—the story goes—

but not a single window cracked, not one.
And the men in the cells were silent.
They heard the volleys. They knew what it meant.
If they wept, they did so alone, to the stones.

Köln Cathedral

Our hearts ring after an hour climb of stone stairs
corkscrewing up a dim spire, no stair younger
than eight hundred years. Bells massive as cars
would frighten even God. How workers hoisted them
to this musty belfry—there's a question for the ages.
Maybe the two boys in Red Sox caps would know.
They smoke in the dark of dust.

Why did generations of souls do it? The boys
go down and we're left alone with the dark, the dust.
Through chinks smaller than postcards, we spy
the brown Rhine, a trestle with a dozen trains,
barges in the distance, black towers of clouds
about to crack in knells of thunder. It had to be
something they believed too deeply to understand.

Back on the wet street I buy a ball point pen.
Köln, Ger., it says and shows a tiny image
of the twin spires where we just were, like gothic
rockets designed in someone's nightmare. Down here,
a red neon sign proclaims IBM the new religion.
Now we're on a train crossing the river,
same train we saw from the spire, same brown Rhine,
same rain, the two black spikes receding on the skyline.

Telescope in the Basement

For Steve and Judy Christenson, and for Linda

It's packed away with its one good eye
in a dark universe, stored in a wooden box
for friends from Montana—
two comets I've lost sight of.

We drove a rutted forest service road
to Cougar Lookout. Judy opened the box,
mounted the long white tube on its tripod.
Steve adjusted the viewfinder,

taught us how to peer without squinting.
Suddenly the setting moon loomed,
its stone face dented, desolate, implacable,
nearly blinding in its hard brightness.

None had seen the moons of Jupiter.
There they were in the scope—
dots of light in line with the larger light.
The Spiral Nebula, though, that was glory,

with no small help from a six-pack.
Stars, telescope, Montana midnight—
moments of bliss are brief,
sweet for that very reason, magnified, often,

by their position in the space of time.
In some other basement—in Great Falls,
maybe, or Boston—molders Steve's panama hat.
A silly straw thing, its ragged brim

somehow right with his red moustache.
Judy aimed the scope at Hercules and said

There's where the cosmos begins.
Beer gave her words a deeper gravity.

Linda spread a tarp on the damp grass.
We four lay in the cool dark
and gave our own names to the glitter,
unaware of the distances to come.

The Aging Body

Strange to see it naked, patched in sunlight
low in the window. Strange to see the knobs
and bulges, the sparse lawn of light hair
on my arms, legs, belly, white on chest, pubis.

This misshapen vessel is me, getting on, as we say,
settling into its final form. I've lived a long time
in its country of peninsulas, rutted roads and outposts.
It's both my frayed suitcase and my rundown hotel.

I'm the night clerk, drowsing at the front desk,
eager for the last guest to vacate, thinking maybe
of joining him for parts unknown, some foreign city
where you hear an accordion after midnight

in the empty piazza, a man singing about love,
about the dolphin spraying water in the fountain,
lit by a square of light from an upper room
where his bed, book and small lamp await him.

Syringa in Twilight

I've dithered away another afternoon.
The sun drops behind a stack of cordwood
vanishing among the white flowers of syringa,
brilliant as white stars clustered in the Seven Sisters.

A stand of aspens loom, barely,
shimmering their way into oblivion
or what passes for oblivion
in this last corner of America—
a bend in the Naches River.

The wind has tapered off.
Syringa flowers recede into the dark
of other shrubs—snowberry, wild rose—
leaving behind the tang
of cinnamon and orange rind.

Across the river,
a light flicks on in an attic room
of the supposedly abandoned Buckeye Ranch.

What became of all the folk singers,
the ones Harry Smith saved from dust?
What became of the scratchy voices
singing about cuckoo birds, murder,
about trying to go home,
sinking in the salt salt sea,
rising to heaven on the wings of a dove?

I've witnessed white flowers massed in green.
I've witnessed light's absence, and now,
in the cool evening, light's return.

BEAUTIFUL PASSING LIVES

When our beach fire had died,
the last embers dimming like stars
and waves clapped and hissed,
quieter on the out tide,

sometime after midnight
we saw on the black horizon
lights of a passenger ship
some five miles off shore,

glide on nothing. No moon.
All those lives, we thought,
those beautiful passing lives.
We must have watched

for an hour the slow constellation
head north, hidden for a time
behind a sea stack, then glittering again
like a better world,

the one we believed would arrive
one day, still on its journey, perhaps,
making only brief appearances,
as comets do, reminding us

of something out there
that may never strike land,
but glitter still, and glide
off shore on nothing.

Why We Hike to the Duck Marsh

Across the road, tadpoles are dancing
On the quarter thumbnail
Of the moon. They can't see.
Not yet.

    —James Wright

REPLACING HER BRAKES
for Linda

She's a good bike mechanic, small box wrench
in hand crouching first in front of the front wheel
to eyeball the alignment, then to the rear
of the rear wheel, studying, tightening,
loosening, since as we know, you do not
want to lose your brakes down a hill at night
in the rain, the busy intersection
of your life at the bottom waiting to see
if you're in control, if you have the touch
so as not to sail through the flashing red light
and open that final door to a field
of crickets rasping in the dark forever.
 No. She has the brake pads in place now,
her face close to check the gap between
rim and rubber. She squeezes each lever,
snaps each cable for tension, and shoves off
for a test ride, the ballet of balance
partnered with angular momentum
as easily as if she were breathing
or talking about why she loves Piaf
or Leonard Cohen. Hallelujah.
Her spokes glint in sunlight, her cheeks
turn rosy with the push of March wind.
Riding a bike is like a certain kind
of conversation with yourself where words
spin freely through the air on the way
to the store or work or a park
or to the village of Beynac carved in rock
above the Dordogne River, where we picnicked
once on the bank, our rented bikes leaning
like lovers against a lamppost on the path.
We marveled at how the river could reflect
the hills, the clear sky, maples flowing
along the shore. We were in love. Still are.

ANOTHER NOTE TO MY SONS

for Devin and Ned

Today we came to a finger stream
where monkey flowers grow

in yellow flarings on the bank.
Sunlight blazed up the grassy slope

of Bethel Ridge. There's a new pond
dammed by sticks

and last year's leaves.
We startled a pair of mergansers.

Such introverts.
They circled above the pines,

then shot upriver
to be, like us, alone.

A young white-tailed doe
stepped out of the trees, stared,

huge ears twitching,
then leaped into the current

in a burst of spray,
crossed and vanished

in a cottonwood thicket.
There used to be a pool

near here, a deep one.
You daredevils would climb

the rock wall, find a ledge,
and jump flailing into that glacial green.

The flood altered it all,
dumped tons of gravel,

dropped a stack of banged up logs.
Willows and serviceberry

hide most of the scars,
the current so gentle now

you'd never believe
it thundered with the clack

of boulders bouncing.
We're well. We shy mergansers

always find a remoter place
to hide and brood.

LAO WANG

She dances now with a billion other Wangs
in the mist over sacred Lao Shan, "Old Mountain."
Her ancestors wrote on tortoise shells.
The character for "water" evolved like water

lilting over stones in the River Li. The word *water*
even sounds like water: *shui,* third or "dipping" tone.
Words can cleanse. She bawled me out once
in country Chinese for not wearing the right clothes

warm enough for a northern China winter.
Squat, bad teeth, bundled in layers of blue cotton,
she's up there bawling out the Yellow Emperor,
she's the aunt I never had, looking out for me,

waiguo ren, "outside country person." How lucky I am
she was cross with the outside country person.
The classroom where I taught was unheated. I chattered
up by the useless blackboard, teaching bored Chinese kids

the wonders of Mary Wollstonecraft's *A Vindication
of the Rights of Women.* Lao Wang, Lao Wang,
I'm not as dumb as I was when you swept our apartment.
I've grown old myself—"Old Ha," my old Chinese friends

would call me, if I had any old Chinese friends.
Ha. Old Ha. Thank you, Lao Wang. *Xiexie.*
One more winter has been given to me, one more chance
to see the Mountain Ash berries turn red.

MOUNTAIN ASH BERRIES

Hard bright clusters hang in the bare tree.
When the boys were boys, we'd cut
quarter inch PVC pipe for blowguns.
It woke you up to catch a berry
in the forehead or neck. But it was war,
and now, robins gather this morning to feed.

How sweet to see myself sprint, crouch,
dodge and aim. *Dad, you're a dead man!*
I see us three in the yard, leaves like years
matted on the lawn—a blur the more I stare.
How sweet the snap of a berry bullet
on the cheek—the sting of living,

a kiss you don't forget. We'd blast
whatever moved, no rules, in late
October light, our tee-shirts grass-grimed,
badged with berry flesh. They moved on,
as kids do. How sweet to be shot,
to die, to come back to life.

SPIDERS, LATE SEPTEMBER

Every morning I destroy their webs,
walking innocently between tomato vines
heavy with red lanterns.

And each night the spiders
undo the damage,
knitting in the dark, repairing again
their intricate scaffolds, and again
I barge through, my bulk erasing their artistry
in all its brilliant utility.

How long do garden spiders live—a month?
To them, I'm a lumbering Cyclops,
a brontosaurus too vast to fathom,
though not as vast as Jehovah,
undoing creation with the flick of a wrist.
To wait, eat and stay alive—
that's the meaning of their ornate weaving,
visible when caught in angled light.

I'm not even sure I can speak of garden spiders
without thinking of life as a quirk—
a lacework so strange it sends a tremor up my spine.
Same chill I feel when webs
brush my bare arm or stick to my cheek.
Beauty is such a fine transparency,
I'm not even sure it exists.

One Less Fall

From here you can smell the age of the year
in the air, its odor of decay, the river sheen
a slurry of cottonwood and pine, hill and sky.

Grass has gone tan on Clemens Ridge,
that slope we always meant to climb
to take in the wider view. *Kingfisher*, you say,

your favorite, chittering upstream, then down,
like we do on our walks, together and alone.
It gets harder, though, to see the end

of earth tones, to face the empty face
of what's to come, where now we're borne
on the river's clatter at this low water time.

You say the boulders look like bones
in the current. Only this late do they emerge
exposed like black eggs, hidden

more often than not, as some thoughts are,
the ones that lie in the deeper channels.
All the summer warblers have flown away:

grosbeak, tanager, siskin—gone.
The land prepares for hard freezes,
then snow, then days of pallid light.

One less fall. Now, though, afternoon sun
reveals more of what we love.
Even a gust of wind that carries the last

papery aspen leaves delivers a swirl of joy.
Some sail all the way across to Old River Road.
Those that light on the river will travel far.

BURROWS MOUNTAIN

for David Long

We haven't been this high since Missoula.
Bud, we're above the trees, worldly concerns,
Rainier's glaciers wrinkled in our faces,
squeezed by pressures we understand too well.

A hundred yards off stand a dozen dirty pillows–
mountain goats–browsing on tundra grass.
So what do we talk about in our rarefied air?
Money. How it guides us up a narrow trail,

how we wish we had some, so we could write
our lives away. My socks hurt.
My camera demands I capture all that glitter.
Through binoculars, we spot specks of climbers

on their afternoon descent from the summit.
They must feel a thrill in their ribs,
having scaled some imagined apex
of their lives. Bud, you and I are in training—

for what, we haven't quite mapped out. Maybe
to do with arriving where we are: this plateau
of gray slate, snow patches, flowers so small
and blue it's a wonder they endure.

A wonder we endure, headed toward the cutoff
of middle age, still fit enough to go part way up
and enjoy the view, the sharp October sun,
each other's aging face, your chapter, my verse.

We promise vaguely to do this again,
get the lungs roaring, calves tight as bowstrings,
sit and watch the younger guys go higher.
We're wiser than they are. We've climbed the ridge

of modest gains, survived the ice of American life,
avalanche of years, and here we are,
feeding sandwich crumbs to a pika who knows
we are tame, knows we could go on,

daylight permitting, if we chose, and gain
another thousand feet to that fist of black basalt.
I'm good right here with you, talking whatever:
money, writing, our kids. I'm good to finger

a green lichen-covered stone, take pictures
of all that glitter, day about done. Bud,
breathe deep. It's time to head back to the city,
our routines, our days of doing what we do.

The Man Who Made My Belt

I meet him in his craft shop in Camden Town.
He's my age, balding, a bit of paunch,
bespectacled, a pale bookworm's face,

eyes that for decades have peered at small things—
the placement of a buckle hole or rivet,
or the smaller holes for a lace to hold together

the gusset of a purse. Mostly, though,
his specialty is leather belts.
He cuts the strips on his long wood table,

gouged in places, blotched with stains on stains—
oxblood, russet, cordovan, buckskin, black—
patches that from my angle look like a biblical sky.

We chat. He asks without looking up and I say,
"From the States," and that's enough for him.
He bends over the table and runs a blade

down the raw grain, then trims the end
of another belt. I pull one from a wooden peg,
admire the diamond pattern dyed brown,

blue and red. He takes my Visa with his stained fingers.
I think of the grave digger who riddles Hamlet
about how long a tanner will last *i' th' earth*.

Nine year. I sign the receipt. He's halved the price
from £20 to £10. "I'm boarding up," he says.
"Poster in the window there. Thirty seven years

I've been at it. John Lennon paid us a visit once."
He has yet to lift his eyes. I see a middling craftsman
plying his trade in a dusty corner, hands scented

with dye, polish, and the older odor of animal hide
that still carries the memory of the body it once housed.
Then: "I'm off to Italy for my final years."

"*Buona fortuna,*" I say and I wonder if he's gotten
news about his heart. First time he's looked up.
Yellow smoker's teeth. Eyes dark like the table

He bends again to his work and says, "Good day."
I pull out my Sears fabric belt and slip in
the new stiff one through the loops—on the snug side—

and step out into the late afternoon London sun,
confident my American jeans will stay put,
less certain about everything else.

LATE MIDDLE AGES

You rise in the dark to make coffee.
I hear the faint clink of a spoon,
cough of the toaster, then nothing,
then the squeak of a faucet,
the sigh of running water.

Your pillow is still warm.
Ten minutes ago you lay
pressed against me, your hand
on my thigh, your breath
shallow as the slow arrival of dawn.

Lines of light form in the drawn blinds.
The front door opens, clicks closed.
Muffled drone of the car pulling away.
I drift in and out. By now
you're in the parking lot,

crossing the frosty asphalt,
about to enter the three story building
where you work,
its face unfathomable,
its upper windows gold

in the sun's just risen fire.
I think of routine partings,
of growing old,
the perfect fit of your breast
in my palm. It grieves me.

Outside the window,
chickadees disagree.
One day one of us
will leave at dawn and not return.
One of us will go to bed alone.

JOCK ITCH

This is the life, La Spezia, July, a cooker.
Even in my tan shorts and sweat-stained
Italia tee shirt, I can almost breathe.

Distant mountains waver in a haze.
What looks like snow, I learn, are bands
of marble, same cream colored stone

laborers hauled to Rome in great slabs.
Sculptors touched and studied and said *Yes!*,
or in the case of a massive flawed block

said *No good. See those unsightly veins?*
Michelangelo bought it for a song and gave us *David*,
naked lad with a sling who takes on a brute

five times his size. I stand outside the door
of a small *farmacia*, rehearsing what I will say
to the wisp of a woman behind the counter.

I know three Italian words—or did know
a minute ago. I'll wait till the shop is empty,
march in and…the tricky part…point to my crotch.

Did David ever deal with this problem?
Maybe I could draw a sketch on the back
of a receipt, add a small arrow to the area

in question. I could say *crea-ma, crea-ma*
and hope there's such a word in Italian.
She looks to be a grandmother. She's seen it all,

including the brute Mussolini, that ranting Cyclops.
Probably she speaks English.
Maybe my three Italian words will sing forth

in an aria of fluency: *per favore, gracie.*
She'll know what I need. She'll know
I'm American, essentially dumb,

passing though her town in some discomfort.
Nothing existential. Just a rawness down below
where life half starts, the place everyone kids about,

the place photographed by millions
in the *Academia* where *David* stands revealed,
coolly sizing up the giant before him,

while the world's travelers and their teenagers
try not to gaze too intently at the beautiful
flawed marble pouch and stem between his legs.

I'll go in and the kind woman
will know immediately what I need
to stop the burning in my groin.

I'll buy a small tube of salve and we'll catch the train
to Vernazza, its pastel hillside houses
sunning themselves above the Mediterranean.

I will be filled with wonder by a patio garden
outside our small *camera*, as though
I've never seen tomatoes or lemons,

or blossoms on the tips of long green zucchini squash.
My love and I will sit on the pier with a bottle
of local white and soak our feet in the sea.

We'll sing the duet from Puccini's little known work
On Top of Old Smokey. And I'll feel fine,
especially down below where it counts.

Abandoned Igloo

for Linda

It looked like a bump in the snow
except for the human roundness,
sun and shadow
patched across its bulge
beneath a stand of lodge pole pines

a mile above Morse Creek.
The narrow descending entry
had stairs, even. Inside,
brighter than we'd expected,
ceiling blocks wedged, somehow,

supported by nothing but gravity
and the designer's gift of balance
and form. Nubs of four red candles,
two at the door, two in ledges hollowed out
above snow benches for sleeping

would have cast amber light.
From without, the dome
would seem to be a kiln
fired in the trees. Two lovers,
we were certain, worked all day

to shape a room of blue cubes.
At night, socked in their down bags,
they read poems aloud—Kinnell, Olds,
Hugo and sweet Jim Wright—
far from the heat of the world.

Why We Hike to the Duck Marsh

For one thing, the ducks. Also,
the flash of redwings in the reeds,
their funny screeching. Across the marsh
a basalt wall climbs a thousand feet,
so there's that. Above it, a cowl of blue
or sometimes a slow train of clouds.

Frogs at dusk. Their earthy songs.
If we sit on a log and wait,
an elk will come to wade the far end.
From inside the rocks, a marmot
will whistle his one long note
about time, space, the risen moon.

August heat brings out sweetness
in the pines. December is good, too,
the pines bearing snow dust
or ice, mallards and buffleheads
keeping open dark ovals
where cattails give cover.

On our first trip, you were large
with our second son. The ground
crunched, frozen along the shore,
edged with fragile floral glass.
Another time—spring it would have been,
aspens just budding—a friend, Jeff,

had died and now that too returns me
to this place of sameness and change.
We've lived a sweet life—a truth
I always forget and must relearn
by repeating the short steep path
that weaves us to our lives like marsh grass.

NOTES

The David Wagoner quote is from his poem "The Words," printed in *Traveling Light: Collected and New Poems*.

The Richard Hugo quote is from *The Triggering Town*.

The William Stafford quote is from *Writing the Australian Crawl*.

The Leslie Marmon Silko quote is from a letter to James Wright, printed in *The Strength and Delicacy of Lace*.

The James Wright quote is from his poem "Small Frogs Killed on the Highway," printed in *Collected Poems*.

ABOUT THE PRESS

The press is named for "Pleasure Boat Studio," an essay written by Ouyang Xiu, Song Dynasty poet, essayist, and scholar, on the twelfth day of the twelfth month in the renwu year (January 25, 1043):

> "I have heard of men of antiquity who fled from the world to distant rivers and lakes and refused to their dying day to return. They must have found some source of pleasure there. If one is not anxious for profit, even at the risk of danger, or is not convicted of a crime and forced to embark; rather, if one has a favorable breeze and gentle seas and is able to rest comfortably on a pillow and mat, sailing several hundred miles in a single day, then is boat travel not enjoyable? Of course, I have no time for such diversions. But since 'pleasure boat' is the designation of boats used for such pastimes, I have now adopted it as the name of my studio. Is there anything wrong with that?"

LaVergne, TN USA
27 December 2010
210152LV00004B/35/P